SPILL *THE* TEA

Unveiling the mysteries of blended, flavored and herbal teas

William Dietz

Spill The Tea: Unveiling The Mysteries Of Blended, Flavored, And Herbal Teas

© 2023 by William Dietz
PO Box 294
St-Eugène, ON, K0B 1P0
Canada

Copyright #1201727—Canadian Intellectual Property Office

All rights reserved.

No part of this book may be reproduced in any form without written permission from the author, except as permitted by Canadian copyright law.

This publication is designed to provide accurate and authoritative information in regard to the subject matter. It is sold with the understanding that the author is not engaged in rendering professional services. While the author has used their best efforts in preparing this book, they make no representations or warranties with respect to the accuracy or completeness of the contents of this book and specifically disclaim any implied warranties of merchantability or fitness for a particular purpose. The advice and strategies contained herein may not be suitable for your situation. You should consult with a professional when appropriate. The author shall not be liable for any loss of profit or any other commercial damages, including but not limited to special, incidental, consequential, personal, or other damages.

Book cover and illustrations by Jen Ashfield
Edited by R5 Website Management

First edition
Paperback ISBN 978-1-7389588-0-1
Electronic book ISBN 978-1-7389588-1-8

PREFACE

This is gross, I thought, as I finished my first sip of the warm, murky beverage. I was fifteen years old and going through a phase where I started to notice my body's reaction to different foods and beverages. Though I was not a full-blown health nut, it looked as if I was headed down that path. I had stopped consuming most sugary drinks and was not fond of taking prescription or over-the-counter drugs. Instead of taking any medicine to relieve my sore throat, at her suggestion, I raided my mother's tea drawer.

Finding the relief I needed, I religiously returned to the tea drawer. I began to enjoy the ritual of preparing tea and quickly fell in love with the flavors. Craving knowledge about this magic elixir, I turned to the internet for a deep dive into the world of tea. My parents had always raised my brother and me to be curious about the world around us. They would go out of their way to provide opportunities to support any interests that caught our attention, no matter how uncommon. Books on tea started to arrive at our door one by one, and I devoured them with a never-ending appetite.

Tea quickly began consuming most of my extracurricular time. One of my favorite resources to quench my thirst for knowledge was online blogs. I followed several and, seeing the passionate community online, was inspired to create my own: Sir William of the Leaf.

One day my parents suggested a trip to Las Vegas so that I could attend a course on tea. They had found educational courses offered by the Specialty Tea Institute (STI). We packed up the car and went off to Vegas. It was a win-win situation for our family: my parents got a two day vacation from their teenagers, and I got a tea class.

Over two days of classes, I was surrounded by tea shop owners, product developers, sales representatives for multinational tea companies, and many others in the tea industry. I do not know if this is what solidified my lifelong career path, but it certainly helped me realize I could make a living as a tea professional.

I built strong connections with the cohort of students moving through the STI courses, and I learned about their various businesses and paths into the professional world of tea. They made a living in tea and loved doing it. That is what I wanted for myself.

At seventeen years old, I was the youngest STI graduate to move through all three levels offered. I started digging to see what path would best position me for a lifelong career in tea. I would have loved a degree in tea, but that was not, and still is not, a track offered by any university in the United States.

One conversation about my future stands out to me. After a tea class, I candidly asked Richard Guzauskas, an instructor for the STI at the time, what he thought would be the best path to enter the tea industry.

The world doesn't need more tea geeks, he said. *It needs more people who understand the business of tea.* He was not downplaying the importance of tea knowledge but rather highlighting that adjacent skills are necessary to make a lucrative career in tea. I owe my deepest gratitude to Richard, who is now my mentor.

I ended up studying marketing and entrepreneurship at Anderson University in Indiana. By sheer coincidence, I met another tea-obsessed student, Chris Bourgea, who operated a small tea business from his dorm room. We quickly connected and I shadowed him for a year to learn about his company. I purchased his tea business following my first year and embarked on my own entrepreneurial journey.

The connections did not stop there. An out-of-the-blue invitation led me to meet Kevin and Skye Huff, an entrepreneurial couple who planned to start a coffee business. Their plan was to expand on my existing network of customers to jumpstart their sales. There was only one problem: I was into tea, not coffee. Luckily I knew a fellow business student, Chris Peterson, who had a background in coffee. After roping him into the venture, we had a complete team. We made the decision to merge the coffee and tea businesses about a year later.

I am admittedly not much of an academic, so leveraging my own entrepreneurial experiences proved the best method to grasp the fundamentals of my business courses. Instead of just accommodating this approach, my professors actually encouraged it. I used my businesses as case studies whenever possible and was even allowed to step out of classes to take sales calls.

PREFACE

I spent my time outside of class learning alongside the team at the coffee company. We all wore many hats in the company, as entrepreneurs do, but I eventually settled into the role of a product developer for both tea and coffee. I was lucky to have the mentorship of seasoned entrepreneurs. That experience taught me as much as my academic studies had.

Graduation was bittersweet since I did not have any leads for positions within the tea industry. I spent the summer of 2014 sending job applications, cold calling various tea professionals, and opening rejection emails. I sent out about four hundred applications, mostly in the tea and coffee industries. Near the end of the summer, I began to get desperate and submitted applications way outside my realm of interest.

I landed an interview with a global beverage company as a sensory analyst for quick-service coffee. It was not ideal, but I did not have an alternative. They offered me the job, and just as I was about to accept, I received a message from Richard Guzauskas, my instructor from the STI. He offered me a chance to interview with DAVIDsTEA as a Tea Blending Apprentice in

Montreal, Canada. This was it! I eagerly accepted the opportunity I had been waiting for.

This experience taught me a key lesson about the tea industry: networking is everything, and maintaining genuine connections leads to great opportunities. The foundation of this book is built on questions about blended and flavored tea collected over several years from my broad network of professionals, hobbyists and consumers. The top recurring themes form the basis of each chapter, and I engage subject matter experts to help paint an accurate portrait of the hidden world of blended and flavored tea.

There are many great books on unflavored, artisanal and single-origin teas, but virtually none on blended tea. I have spent the past fifteen years studying all facets of tea, but the sparse amount of published information about blended and flavored tea that does exist is either outdated or inaccurate. Throughout my career, the door was opened to learning about blended and flavored tea, but for anyone without an inside connection, it is impossible to find the true answers about blended tea. Until now. This book is the window to that hidden world.

1

COMMUNITY, RIVALRY AND PASSION

There is no bad tea... Yes, I said it. I know this is a highly controversial thing to say, but I believe that understanding and accepting this fact will help elevate the tea industry worldwide.

Why do I say there is no bad tea? Because regardless of whether a company sells straight tea, blended, or flavored tea, there is a market for it. Some consumers value the most rare single-origin teas available, while others are happy to sip on a comforting Earl Grey from their local grocery store.

Expert tasters have a multitude of adjectives to describe the taste, processing method, or leaf style (a descriptor pertaining to size, shape, or other physical attributes of the tea leaves or other ingredients). However, there is a market for every tea, even those that tasters deem inferior.

Quality is relative to the price consumers are willing to pay.

This is something I have learned on my tea journey from blogger to professional, and it has aided my understanding of how to make objective decisions and recommendations when evaluating teas and blends. Blended tea differs from straight tea in that the latter contains only one ingredient: processed leaves of the Camellia Sinensis plant. Blended tea, however, can be composed of multiple kinds of tea or contain various herbs, fruits, spices, and flavors. Throughout this book, the terms 'blended tea' and 'flavored tea' will be used interchangeably.

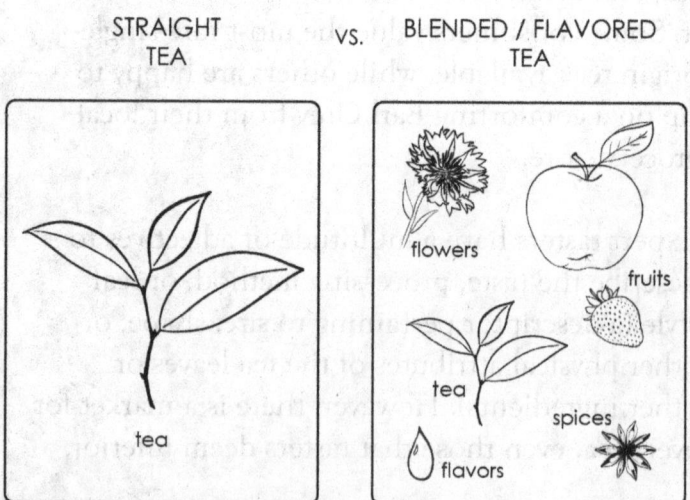

Whether you are an entrepreneur, employee, hobbyist, or passionate consumer, there will be takeaways in this book that will direct your journey in tea. My goal is to empower you to view teas objectively within the context of the blended tea industry as a whole.

EVERY TEA HAS A DESTINATION

I remember the first time I went to Sri Lanka to visit the tea gardens and factories. I tasted through multitudes of different samples at several factories and at a tea brokerage firm. These teas came from every kind of tea garden across the island, and they all tasted different. I got to take part in tasting tea at each step of production, and it was an eye-opening experience. I tasted dust, stems, twigs, and even teas deemed defective. Defects can happen during processing that cause the leaf to taste smokey, flat, or under-oxidized.

These were not teas that I was seeking out for DAVIDsTEA, but all were ultimately sold to someone. I was surprised because I had never seen these tea grades on the general market. I learned they are typically favored in countries where there is less disposable income. Every grade of tea coming out of the factories, even those deemed defective, were purchased by companies intent on making them into blends their customers would love.

This is where I learned that there's no such thing as bad tea. Quality is relative to the customer drinking it, in terms of both flavor profile and cost.

Oftentimes people start out drinking blended tea because it is easy and, arguably, more accessible. Straight tea can be intimidating, with ethereal descriptions of taste or hard to understand processing methods. In contrast, a black tea with strawberry flavoring may be more relatable and comfortable.

There are many habitual tea drinkers who will sip on flavored hot water steeped from inexpensive tea bags every day simply out of habit. They have made it a part of their lives and their day does not feel complete without it.

These habitual tea drinkers generally begin their tea journey by drinking blended teas. Most people do not start their tea journey with specialty straight tea, as blended tea is a perfect gateway into the world of tea. The majority of people I know in the tea community began by sipping regularly on classic breakfast blends or Earl Grey, a heritage blend of black tea flavored with a citrus fruit called bergamot.

Straight tea enthusiasts are looking for what they consider to be an elevated drinking experience. They do not want what they perceive as tea bag dust that has been swept off the factory floor and instead seek higher quality, single origin, and small batch teas which exemplify a specific style of tea, growing region, or the craft of the tea maker.

Neither the habitual tea bag customer nor the straight tea enthusiast is wrong in their choices. The tea industry needs all types of consumers to continue to grow. I have learned in this business that there is a market for all types of teas.

I work in blend development for the company, DAVIDsTEA, and have tasted several thousand different teas and blends. There have been many teas that I did not personally enjoy but felt would be a good fit for DAVIDsTEA's customers. I have also tasted blends that had great flavor balance and were creative but did not fit into the company's market.

If you come into the industry with the attitude that there is only one correct way to make tea, it will perpetuate the rivalry between straight tea and blended tea drinkers and hinder the growth of the tea community.

STRAIGHT TEA VERSUS BLENDED TEA

What causes the rivalry between straight tea and blended tea? Among many industry professionals and enthusiasts, straight tea is highly regarded because, to some, it offers a superior drinking experience. A company may want customers to gradually start drinking these types of straight teas but it is unlikely they will start there since blended tea serves as a better gateway into the world of tea, offering consumers more relatable flavors. Blended tea is important to the development of the straight tea industry because it is often a customer's first experience.

As with wine, you do not usually start buying rare, unfiltered bottles from Italy right away. You work your way there over time. There is a progression that takes place with wine drinking, and the same is true with tea. The term I use for people who start drinking blended tea and move to straight tea is graduation. It describes the customer's behavior.

This behavior mirrors my own tea journey. I started as a tea blogger and hobbyist under the pen name Sir William of the Leaf. I first started drinking blended tea but moved away from that to drinking straight tea. It was interesting to me how a single leaf could take on so many different flavors.

I know many people in the tea business who look down on blended tea and, admittedly, I held that same attitude as a tea blogger. Tea enthusiasts and professionals can both be snobbish when it comes to their reverence for straight teas.

My belief now is that it is imperative for the industry to recognize the vital role that blended teas play in growing tea consumption worldwide. Everyone in the tea industry should be holding hands and working together to grow. Why would you shun or disrespect this perceived other side if they are helping to grow your business? If more people are drinking tea, everyone will prosper.

COMMUNITY AND PASSION

My hope is that the industry becomes more community focused so that everyone within it grows. A spirit of comradery already exists in the industry, and tea is the driving passion that brings us together.

Trade shows and expositions feel like big family reunions. Once you get into the industry, you will likely make fast friends with suppliers, enthusiasts, and even competitors. This network is vital to maintaining the core passion and aligning everyone towards one mission-bringing tea to the forefront of the beverage industry.

The specialty tea business is not a huge money making industry. It makes money as a commodity, but for the most part, people do not go into this business to get rich. Though growing, it is small compared to the several billion dollar coffee industry.

Inherent passion for tea as a product is a driving force for many to start a tea business. They come to love tea and the way it makes them feel when exploring tastes or sharing the excitement with others. It is an enriching trade!

If you meet someone who is interested in tea, they will want to introduce you to new flavors and products. Suppliers have sent samples to me that they knew I would not purchase, but simply because they were excited to share them personally.

We are all deeply passionate about this industry. It is why we dedicate ourselves to it every day and why we invite people to experience it with us.

I sat down with my friend Kevin Gascoyne, the co-founder of Camellia Sinensis, and we talked about this intrinsic desire to share our love of tea and build community. He is known for hosting tea events and tea nights when he invites others to bring any tea and sit around to share ideas, often into the wee hours of the night. Here is what he said about the community of the tea industry:

Few people would drift towards tea as a big money making venture. Most of us come to this industry as hobbyists with a certain level of passion for the product. There are plenty more profitable entrepreneurial ventures if money were the focus. I manage to pay the rent by peddling tea now, but just as with many of us, it started as an obsessive hobby.

This shared enthusiasm and passion for the product gives us plenty of common ground, makes it pleasurable to hang out with people from other tea companies, and nourishes this sense of community.

Thus, the regular hosting of tea nights to focus on the enjoyment of good leaf in good company. The tea gradually stimulates our minds and soothes our bodies, flavor profiles are explored and ideas exchanged. The great vibe to share with fellow enthusiasts.

We regularly have friends from multiple tea companies sitting around the table just talking about tea ... not business. It is quite a unique situation when compared to the shark-filled waters of other commodity industries.

For newcomers to the industry, there are great advantages to reaching out to other tea companies. Most will be helpful with feedback and do what they can to help. I have helped many start-up tea companies in one way or another over the years.

One evening, during a tea session, an enthusiastic friend mentioned how surprised he was to be sitting at a table with six different tea companies. But in this industry, it is not uncommon to purchase from many different companies.

In my experience, most companies will be open and generous with such advice and guidance. Tea is a growing industry, so there is less of the tight, claustrophobic feel that some other industries have. There is still room for more participants.

The rivalry between straight tea and flavored blends is natural. A certain number of the tea drinking population will go down the road to focus on single origin teas.

As with any hobby, their enthusiasm, especially at first, may focus on the peripheral elements of preparation techniques and the ritual of drinking artisanal tea in traditional ways. It can become a form of identification, in some cases, an unnecessary elitism over other products and infusions. It is true that the subtlety and purity of unblended products, once it becomes your focus, can make it tough to appreciate anything else but not to the point we need to be putting down others' preferences or the products that meet their budgets.

We prefer to put forward the concept that tea is a noble product from top to bottom. It is a 5,000 year old health tonic that will improve your day and your life. Whatever the flavor complexity or finesse, in the end, it is all still tea.

GROWING TOGETHER

I agree with Kevin on this, and many people in the industry feel the same way. We have a strong community that is happy to help newcomers, for the most part.

One thing that I appreciate about Kevin is that he is happy I work for DAVIDsTEA. He told me that he had gained so many more customers simply because DAVIDsTEA was attracting more tea drinkers. This growth is ultimately beneficial for all tea merchants.

More often than not, everyone is here to cultivate growth and support the industry. The spirit of competition tends to be different even though we can not be naive and say it is nonexistent. Many tea organizations across the world provide resources and educational programs on various facets of tea, so there is no shortage of, or limited access to information, with the exception of flavored tea.

While visiting one of DAVIDsTEA's suppliers during a development trip, I discovered that a representative from a competitive company was in the tasting room next door. I passed him in the hallway and he introduced himself.

Then he did the most surprising thing I could have imagined and invited me to see what they were working on. I tasted their blends, gave my comments, and we even shared lunch together.

It was a fascinating experience. Technically, we were competitors, but that did not stop him from inviting me to take part in the passion we both shared. Thinking back on this, I can not fathom it being commonplace in other industries where fierce competition exists. We did not steal each other's ideas as it would not have been beneficial for our individual customer bases. Instead, we set aside any perceived rivalry and openly exchanged our knowledge, strengthening the community of the tea industry and demonstrating our shared passion.

2
FLAVORING

Liquid flavoring is NOT flavoring oil. If you did not know that, you are not alone. Many people in the tea industry refer to flavoring as oil, even if they are a veteran of the industry. This is just one of the countless pieces of misinformation about what flavoring is, how it is made, and how it is applied to tea.

Accurate information on flavor is hard to find. This is true even outside of the tea industry. If you have ever flipped over a bag of chips, a package of cookies, or just about any food product, you will likely have seen "flavoring" in the ingredient list without any additional explanation. Even the most reputable tea suppliers have muddy information regarding flavoring, but it is not their fault. Flavoring in the food and beverage industry is shrouded in mystery because the manufacturing industry thrives on secrecy.

However, there is a beacon of hope for clarity.

development and manufacturing, and lobbies governments for certain laws and protections in order to protect the fruits of their labor. This gives them leeway to use different ingredients to make flavoring, and to swap ingredients without significant changes to labeling that would impact the entire consumer packaged goods industry.

In full disclosure, flavoring is used at such a small percentage in tea blends that there are literally trace amounts that end up in a cup of tea. Flavoring usually composes anywhere between 0.25% - 5% of the overall weight of a blended tea before it is steeped. The flavor chemical compounds are so intense and volatile that even a tiny amount can have a big impact. Remember, steeped tea is approximately 98% water.

COMMON QUESTIONS ABOUT FLAVORING

I received several similar inquiries about flavoring as part of my initial questionnaire. In this chapter, we will answer the most common consumer and professional questions with the help of Glenn Kraemer from McCormick FONA.

There are a few industry experts who are willing to offer transparent information. I interviewed a flavor chemist from McCormick FONA, based in Geneva, Illinois, on sharing real information about flavoring in the tea industry and to answer the pertinent questions asked by customers and merchants alike.

I first became aware of McCormick FONA in 2013 while still in university and working with a tea and coffee startup in central Indiana. I was primarily involved in the development of roast profiles for coffee, new tea blends, and their signature flavored coffees. My ever-supportive parents sent me a link to sign up for flavor classes offered by McCormick FONA. Of course, I jumped on the opportunity to learn from industry experts and to geek out about flavoring.

The classes I took gave me a foundation of knowledge that I later realized was rare among tea industry experts. I was surprised that peop' who had been blending tea for a few decades were unaware of this knowledge. This is no of ignorance in the tea industry. It is the f' industry that clouds this information.

The flavor industry invests huge resou

FLAVORING

Glenn is a flavor chemist, also known as a flavorist, and has been in the industry for over 14 years. His job is to make food products taste better through the use of flavors. His answers are clear and straightforward as he debunks myths and corrects the misinformation surrounding flavoring. Flavoring is used in just about every food and beverage application out there, from sweet treats to salty snacks.

Here are the questions asked during the interview:

1. What is flavoring made of?
2. What are the differences between natural and artificial flavors?
3. What are the differences between flavors and essential oils?
4. Why is the smell of flavored tea different from the taste?
5. What is the purpose of flavoring?
6. How is flavoring applied to tea?

1. WHAT IS FLAVORING MADE OF?

Everything on this earth is made of chemicals, from fields of wildflowers to the gasoline you put in your car. The best place to start explaining what flavoring is made of is by tasting a freshly picked strawberry. This strawberry may contain thousands of different chemicals that impact its color, flavor, and aroma, but only a few hundred contribute to each attribute. Within those few hundred chemicals, it is likely that only half are immediately recognized by our noses and taste buds. It is those select chemicals that are used to develop strawberry flavors.

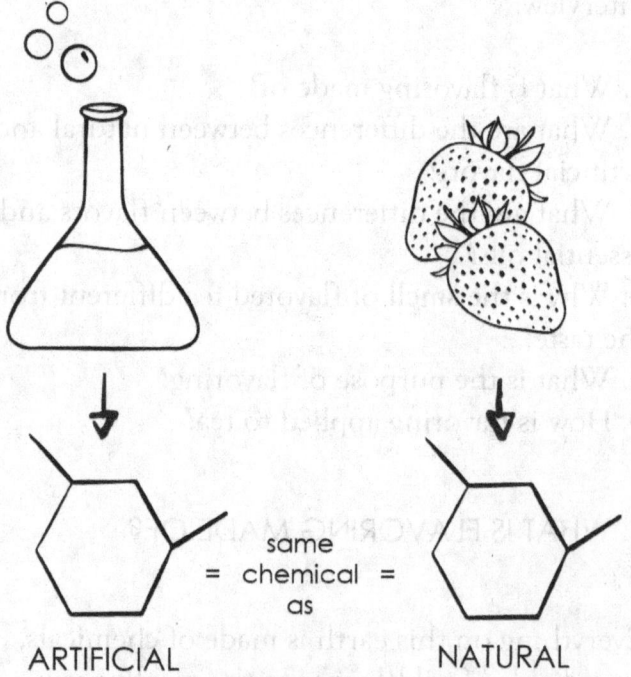

Chemicals are the main component of flavoring. Whether in solid or liquid form, they can be extracted from natural sources, synthesized in a lab, or a combination of both. The chemicals are mixed with food-safe solvents that help distribute them into the desired application. The Food and Drug Administration defines flavor as follows:

The term 'artificial flavor' or 'artificial flavoring' means any substance, the function of which is to impart flavor, which is not derived from a spice, fruit or fruit juice, vegetable or vegetable juice, edible yeast, herb, bark, bud, root, leaf or similar plant material, meat, fish, poultry, eggs, dairy products, or fermentation products thereof.

The term 'natural flavor' or 'natural flavoring' means the essential oil, oleoresin, essence or extractive, protein hydrolysate, distillate, or any product of roasting, heating or enzymolysis, which contains the flavoring constituents derived from a spice, fruit or fruit juice, vegetable or vegetable juice, edible yeast, herb, bark, bud, root, leaf or similar plant material, meat, seafood, poultry, eggs, dairy products, or fermentation products thereof, whose significant function in food is flavoring rather than nutritional.

https://www.accessdata.fda.gov/scripts/cdrh/cfdocs/cfcfr/cfrsearch.cfm?fr=501.22

2. WHAT ARE THE DIFFERENCES BETWEEN NATURAL AND ARTIFICIAL FLAVORS?

Believe it or not, molecularly speaking, the chemicals are identical between natural and artificial flavors. The flavors could be derived or synthesized through a natural extraction process. An orange flavor, for example, could be created synthetically in a lab from artificial components, but the molecular structure of the chemicals is the same as what you might derive from a real orange. Those chemicals are no different than the natural chemicals that give an orange its distinct flavor and aroma.

One reason flavoring manufacturers may rely on synthetic or artificial flavors is that there is a limited amount of any given material found in nature. Since some materials are so sparse, it can be cost-prohibitive to derive the flavor from natural sources. Another reason is to minimize impurities. Flavors are made up of a few select chemicals from any given source, so flavor manufacturers need to isolate those specific chemicals. Extracting these from multiple sources usually brings a slew of unwanted chemicals that need further processing to eliminate. Synthetic flavors help reduce the risk of impurities in the final product.

FLAVORING

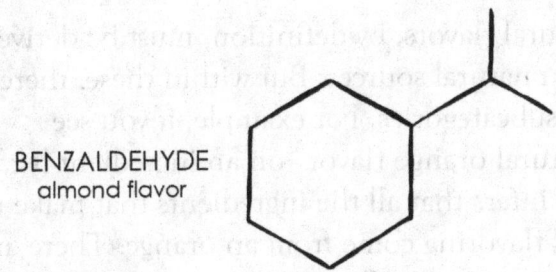

BENZALDEHYDE
almond flavor

Benzaldehyde is the main component in almond flavor. It can be synthesized or extracted from a variety of sources.

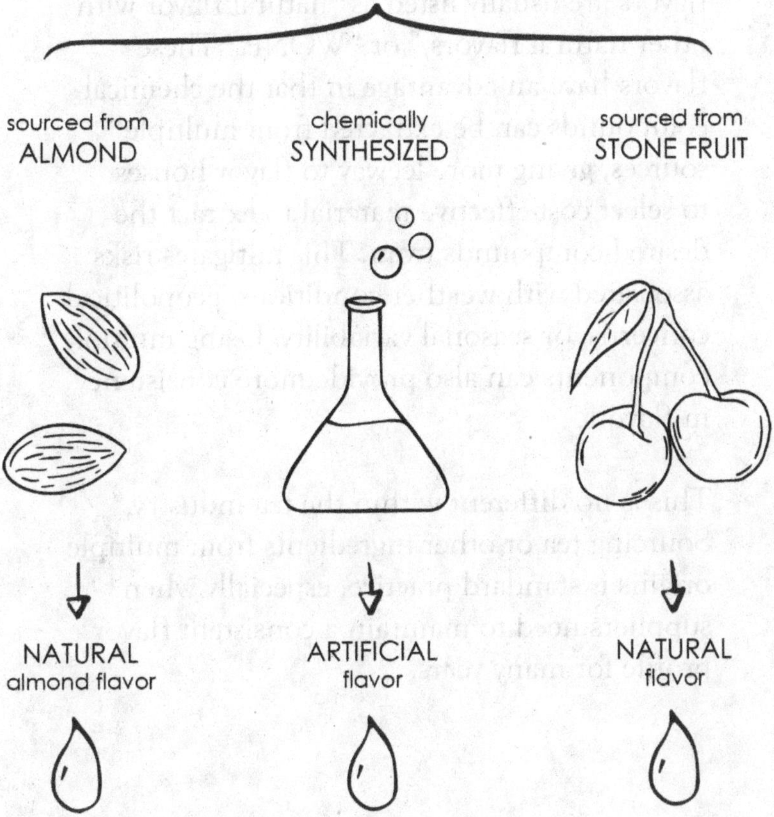

sourced from	chemically	sourced from
ALMOND	**SYNTHESIZED**	**STONE FRUIT**

NATURAL	**ARTIFICIAL**	**NATURAL**
almond flavor	flavor	flavor

Natural flavors, by definition, must be derived from natural sources. But within these, there are subcategories. For example, if you see "natural orange flavor" on an ingredient list, this infers that all the ingredients that make up that flavoring come from an orange. There are also orange-type flavors that may give a similar taste but could be derived from limes, lemons, or any combination of natural sources. These flavors are usually listed as "natural flavor with other natural flavors," or "WONF." These flavors have an advantage in that the chemical compounds can be extracted from multiple sources, giving more leeway to flavor houses to select cost-effective material to extract the desired compounds from. This mitigates risks associated with weather conditions, geopolitical concerns, or seasonal variability. Using multiple components can also provide more consistency in flavors.

This is no different within the tea industry. Sourcing tea or other ingredients from multiple origins is standard practice, especially when suppliers need to maintain a consistent flavor profile for many years.

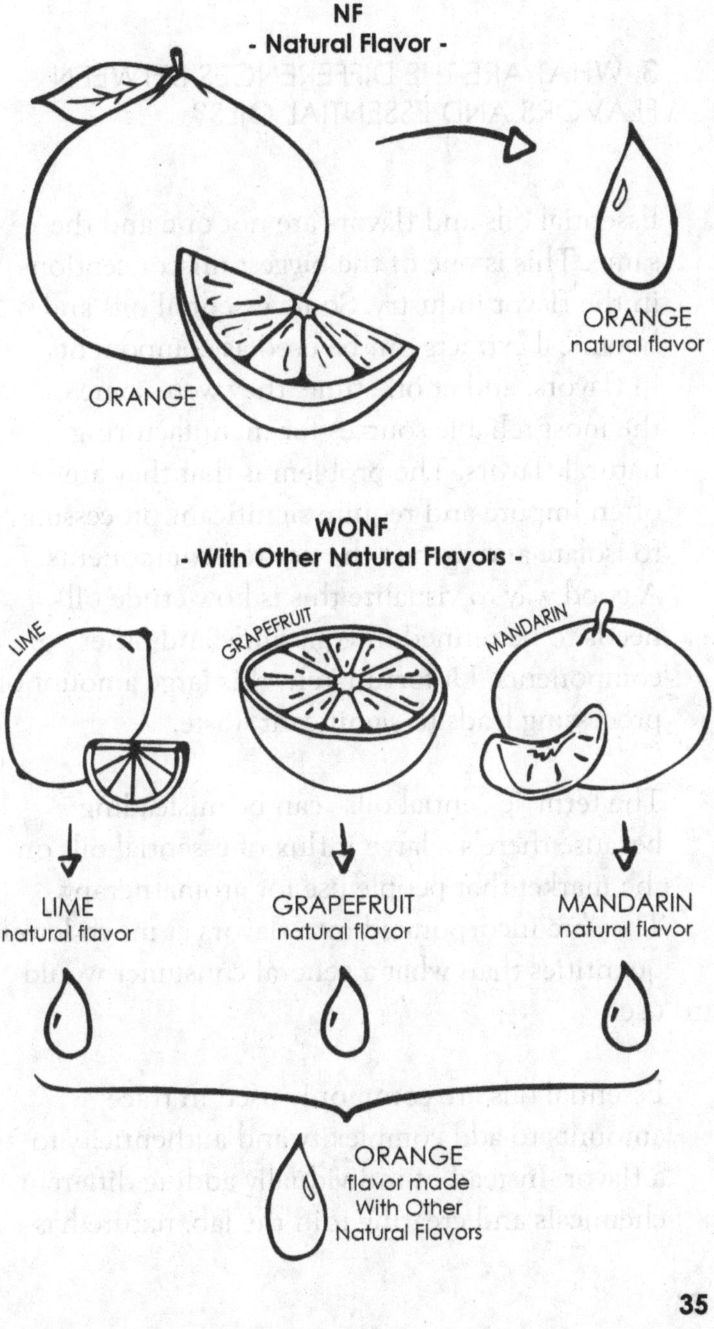

FLAVORING

NF
- Natural Flavor -

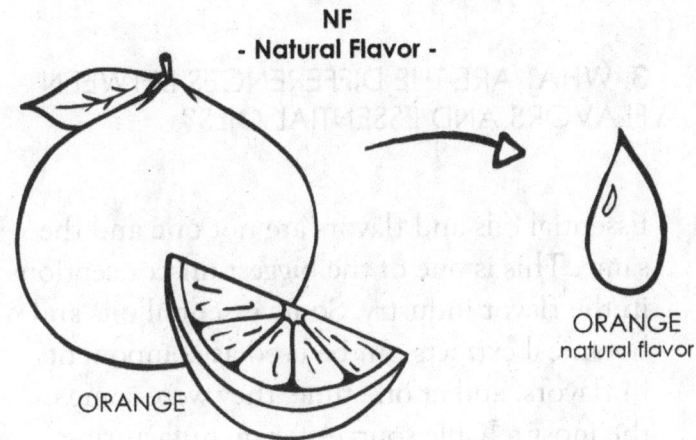

ORANGE

ORANGE
natural flavor

WONF
- With Other Natural Flavors -

LIME

GRAPEFRUIT

MANDARIN

LIME
natural flavor

GRAPEFRUIT
natural flavor

MANDARIN
natural flavor

ORANGE
flavor made
With Other
Natural Flavors

3. WHAT ARE THE DIFFERENCES BETWEEN FLAVORS AND ESSENTIAL OILS?

Essential oils and flavors are not one and the same. This is one of the biggest misconceptions in the flavor industry. Some essential oils and botanical extracts can be used as components in flavors, and at one time, they were some of the most reliable sources for manufacturing natural flavors. The problem is that they are often impure and require significant processing to isolate and extract the desired components. A good way to visualize this is how crude oil needs to be refined into gasoline and other components. Unfortunately, this large amount of processing leads to significant waste.

The term "essential oils" can be misleading because there's a large influx of essential oils on the market that people use for aromatherapy. They are incorporated into flavors at much lower quantities than what a general consumer would use.

Essential oils are commonly used in trace amounts to add complexity and authenticity to a flavor. Instead of individually adding different chemicals and creating it in the lab, nature has already provided a ratio that can be trusted to replicate an aroma or flavor.

One thing commonly said in the tea industry is that flavoring is an oil, which is not necessarily true. Some flavors are oil soluble, but predominantly water soluble flavors are used in the tea industry since the majority of people steep their tea in water. Oil soluble flavors are more commonly used in the production of coffee. It is a common practice to mix freshly roasted coffee beans with oil soluble flavoring, but not typically in the tea industry.

4. WHY IS THE SMELL OF FLAVORED TEA DIFFERENT FROM THE TASTE?

The best place to start in answering this question is to understand the difference between flavor and taste. Flavors are closely linked with aromas. A person's retronasal olfactory glands help in perceiving the flavors, or more accurately, the aromas of food and drinks. These volatile chemical compounds are recognized by your brain when you inhale, whether through your nose or mouth.

SPILL THE TEA

The experience of taste is linked with saltiness, bitterness, acidity (sourness), sweetness, and umami (savoriness). Incorporating the bitterness and astringency of tea, especially camellia sinensis, with the aroma compounds in flavoring, creates a unique flavor experience. Flavors will react differently when applied to various fruits, herbs, or even confections. Flavorists need to match the right type of flavoring to the intended application. For example, they may recommend using a powdered, oil soluble flavoring for a boxed cake mix.

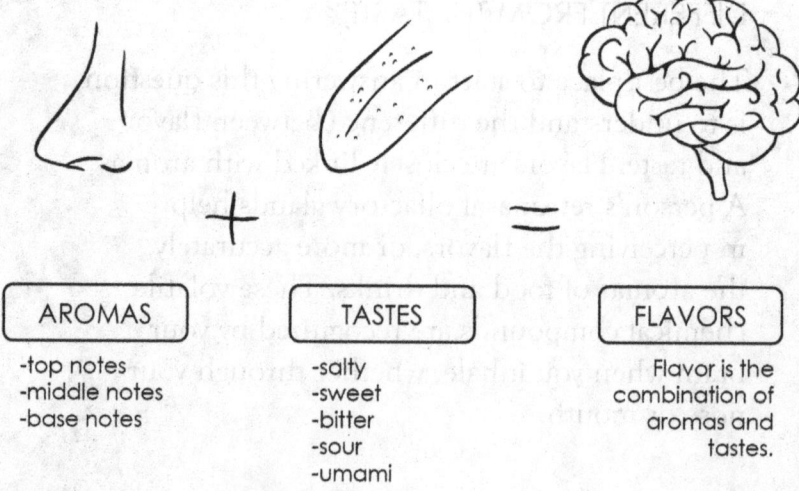

AROMAS	TASTES	FLAVORS
-top notes -middle notes -base notes	-salty -sweet -bitter -sour -umami	Flavor is the combination of aromas and tastes.

FLAVORING

Another part of why the smell of tea and the taste can differ is due to the drinking experience itself. Flavorists tend to break up flavors into a triangle made up of base notes, mid notes, and top notes. When developing flavors, they try to incorporate chemicals in such a way that they are well balanced. Balancing these notes is vital for tea since heat will cause certain volatile top notes to rise to the top and hit your nose first.

Usually, a consumer does not want the first sip of something to overwhelmingly taste of one top note in the flavor, as this could be unpleasant. On the other extreme, they do not want the lingering back notes of the flavor to stay in their mouth for too long. Neither of these situations creates a positive drinking experience. Again, it is all about balance.

Flavor houses have teams of people dedicated to working on a specific application for each flavor. This is why it is important to work with flavor houses to customize flavors that best fit the intended end use. It is up to the scientist in the lab that specializes in tea flavor application to know exactly what needs to be done to get the flavor and aroma to match. This is extremely customizable, and the ratios of chemicals within the flavor are paramount to good development. A reputable flavor house should have experts in flavor application for dry tea and blends.

I asked Glenn to share his insights on how flavors differ from region to region. The blended tea industry is primarily centered in Germany, and many flavors there are different from what my North American tuned palate expected.

He said that one of the best examples of this that comes to mind is root beer. In North America, the smell of root beer is something people enjoy because it is a popular soft drink flavor. However, in Europe, the smell of root beer is associated with dirty locker rooms because sports teams use sarsaparilla scented products to reduce inflammation. Commercial root beer is no longer made with sarsaparilla as recently there have been health concerns over people consuming the root. The flavor is primarily derived from wintergreen now.

Licorice is another great example. North Americans associate licorice with anise-type flavors, especially in confections like black licorice candies. Europeans tend to associate it more with actual licorice root. Flavor companies should have a sensory department that runs tests to determine whether or not a specific flavor will resonate with the intended target audience.

Another key area to consider for a flavoring supplier is the food safety laws and labeling regulations of each country they manufacture in or sell to. Flavors that are considered natural in some countries might not be considered natural elsewhere, so it is important to work with a flavor house that knows these requirements. A good tea supplier should share this information and understand how each flavor needs to be labeled in the intended country of sale.

5. WHAT IS THE PURPOSE OF FLAVORING?

Consumers and people outside of the flavoring industry may think that the manufacturers in the flavoring industry are trying to deceive or trick them. McCormick FONA is committed to transparency and offers a solid understanding of the rather mysterious words "natural flavor" and "artificial flavor." McCormick FONA's Flavor University helps educate people as to what these ingredients are, why they exist, and how they function.

The main purpose of flavoring is to help create a consistent, great tasting product that has a long shelf life. Flavor chemicals in fresh foods are volatile and degrade quickly. The food and beverage industry is able to capture these compounds and introduce them into products so they can be enjoyed longer, with a flavor intensity similar to the real thing.

This means they can also introduce flavors into products that otherwise could not have certain flavors. Flavorists can not pump chewing gum full of orange juice and expect to have an orange flavored chewing gum. Orange juice is mostly water, so this could not possibly work. This is only possible through the magic of flavors. Flavoring allows consumers access to better variety and stability in their food and beverage options.

Surprisingly, sustainability is a little known aspect of flavoring. The discarded materials from orange juice manufacturers are one of the primary source materials used to create orange flavoring. After the manufacturers are done squeezing the oranges, flavorists can extract the leftovers and get the chemicals needed to create flavors. This is a standard industry practice and has been done since long before manufacturers put an emphasis on sustainability initiatives.

The demand for good tasting products exceeds the supply that is able to be grown or made. That is one of the main benefits of the flavoring industry: they can find ways to deliver that satisfaction with less environmental impact.

6. HOW IS FLAVORING APPLIED TO TEA?

Flavorings can be used alone or in combinations to create appropriate flavor profiles that will suit consumer tastes. The direction could be as straightforward as a citrus, or as complex as strawberry cheesecake with rosemary.

It is not as simple as one may think. Creating a strawberry black tea is not always as easy as applying strawberry flavoring on a black tea. There are tons of factors to consider. For example, there are many different types of strawberry flavoring. Maybe you want more of a fresh strawberry flavor. Or you may be looking for a jam type of flavor. What about a candy type strawberry? The ingredients used to create these differences are complex and require blending. You will likely have to source different flavors and combinations to achieve a desired flavor profile, and it could even be that those flavors will not include strawberries at all.

A good example of this is a blueberry tea blend that was carried by DAVIDsTEA. It required both blueberry and raspberry flavoring to create that flavor profile. The blueberry flavor gave the familiar floral and fresh blueberry note to the blend, but the specific raspberry flavor used lent a jammy, fruity sweetness. Even though the blend was not marketed as raspberry, it would not have been the same without that key flavor.

Tea blenders will normally make small, hand blended samples when testing flavorings on various tea bases. These samples are anywhere from 25 to 100 grams and represent what the large production blend will taste like. All the ingredients, including flavoring, are weighed out according to the recipe and mixed either in a bag, bowl, or even on cardstock. It is then tasted and evaluated like any other tea.

Several types of machines can blend large amounts of tea, and flavoring is introduced according to the capability of the machine. This can be as simple as pouring the liquid flavor or flavor granules into a rotating drum, or it can be injected via nozzles that spray the flavor onto the blend as it is mixing. This is to ensure even coverage so that every cup of tea is consistent.

WHAT IS ONE OF THE MOST SURPRISING FACTS ABOUT FLAVORING?

I ended my interview with Glenn by asking him what is one of the most surprising facts about flavoring.

One of the most surprising things people learn is that organic certified flavors are not what they seem. Flavorists are using natural botanicals and organic certified botanicals as their raw materials, but they can blend them in a beaker in the lab to create an organic flavor. This can be a confusing concept for many people, as the perception is anything certified organic has to come directly from the soil. These flavors undergo a couple of extra steps that are necessary for organic certification, but they are still manufactured and processed in labs like any other type of flavor.

FLAVORING IS ESSENTIAL

I need to reiterate the point that flavoring is a vital part of the food and beverage industry. It is important that people are aware of all facets of flavoring, regardless of the values of any given brand. Even if that brand's customers only value natural flavoring, it does not mean others should shun artificial flavors. Artificial flavors are still a valuable part of the tea industry.

Equipping yourself with knowledge and understanding will benefit everyone in the tea industry. I highly recommend that anyone active in the tea industry consider taking classes from McCormick FONA or other reputable sources. Doing so will help curb the spread of misinformation about the ingredients found in tea blends, and that knowledge will help us all.

3

THE JOURNEY OF BLENDED TEA

A customer walks into a tea shop and asks, "Where does this tea come from?" It seems like a simple question, and in most cases, it is. Uncovering the origin of straight tea is relatively straightforward. Questions can be answered by stating the country, region, garden, or any combination of these. Is blended tea this simple? What is the story behind the ingredients you find in your cup?

Is there an easy answer to the consumer's question? Not entirely. The story goes something like this: the black tea in the blend might come from India, the apples could come from Turkey, the flower petals may come from Albania, and the flavoring from Switzerland. Depending on the labeling laws in the country of sale, the package might say "Product of Germany."

Why is the source of your tea important? Because many of the top consumer questions I received during my initial research for this book were related to origin and supply chain transparency. Here are a few of the questions I received:

- Where is the tea grown?
- Where is the tea blended?
- Where are the ingredients from?
- Are the ingredients sourced locally?

Tea drinkers care where the ingredients in their cup come from. The following information will shed light on the complex supply chain of blended tea and bring transparency to the factors contributing to it.

The story of each blended tea is not going to be as simple as "this tea comes from India or China." Rather, the individual ingredients are sourced from around the world and come together under one roof to be transformed into something greater than the sum of its parts.

The blended and flavored tea industry is highly consolidated to a handful of large manufacturers primarily in Europe and North America. The industry is tight-knit, and the blenders amass hundreds of ingredients from every corner of the world, producing thousands of blends for clients spanning the globe.

THE JOURNEY OF BLENDED TEA

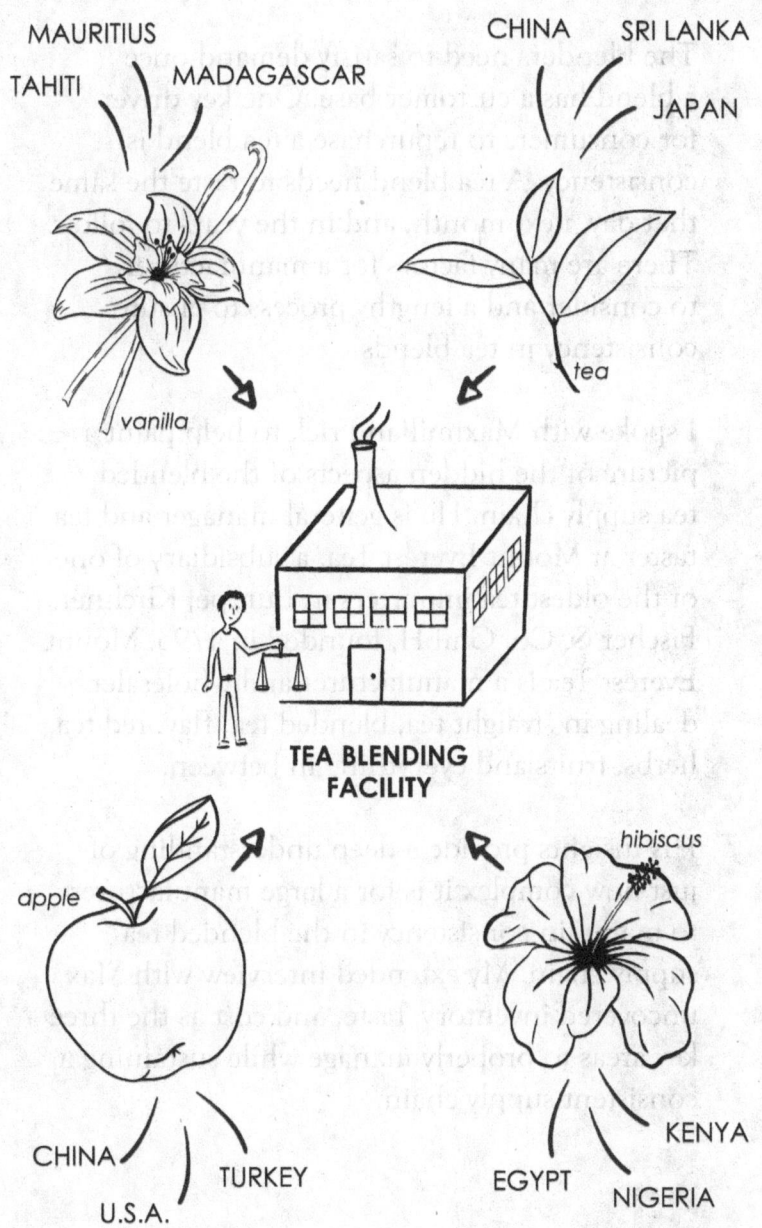

The blenders need to satisfy demand once a blend has a customer base. One key driver for consumers to repurchase a tea blend is consistency. A tea blend needs to taste the same that day, next month, and in the years to follow. There are many factors for a manufacturer to consider and a lengthy process to ensure consistency in tea blends.

I spoke with Maximilian Frick to help paint a picture of the hidden aspects of the blended tea supply chain. He is general manager and tea taster at Mount Everest Tea, a subsidiary of one of the oldest tea importers in Europe, Kirchner, Fischer & Co. GmbH, founded in 1793. Mount Everest Tea is a manufacturer and wholesaler dealing in straight tea, blended tea, flavored tea, herbs, fruits and everything in between.

His insights provide a deep understanding of just how complex it is for a large manufacturer to maintain consistency in the blended tea supply chain. My extended interview with Max uncovered inventory, taste, and cost as the three key areas to properly manage while sustaining a consistent supply chain.

CONSISTENCY IN INVENTORY

The first image that comes to mind when you think of tea is probably not Germany. Yet, Germany exports a significant amount of tea and has been doing so for centuries. In the historic port of Hamburg, you will see vast rows of red brick buildings bordering a series of canals. Several stories high, cranes jut out over the water. While they are not in use today, these cranes were once at the heart of Germany's massive commodity trading industry.

Direct port access was a key advantage to the success of the trading industries there. Coffee, spices, tea, rugs and other foreign goods still pass through the old port to this day. Commodity trading is a legacy industry, and some of the tea blenders have been operating in northern Germany since the 1700's.

German engineering also plays a key role in the blended tea industry. Maintaining intricate machines and complex manufacturing processes are barriers to entry for many. The machines require a large capital investment in equipment and in people to operate and repair them. Germany has a large talent pool specializing in manufacturing technology.

According to Max:

The focus Germany has always had on trade, combined with the experience that people have in the industry, has caused them to be a leader in the market. They have continued to show that they are doing it right and have kept up with the changes in the tea industry along the way.

What does all this have to do with maintaining consistent inventories of ingredients? Port access and a firm foundation in commodity trading have sprouted a solid network of large tea suppliers in a focused region. Their combined efforts over hundreds of years helped to put in place a streamlined process for importing and exporting teas, herbs and blended products on a huge scale.

A large tea blender may need to maintain an inventory of 600-1,000 different ingredients sourced from 30-40 countries. And at any given time, they may need to alter their supply chain based on availability of those ingredients, costs, or any number of other factors. Adaptability is necessary to maintain a consistent supply of ingredients, even to the point that tea blenders may buy from each other when in a pinch.

Given this complexity, one can imagine that a simple question regarding the origin of a blended tea is anything but simple.

CONSISTENCY IN TASTE

Once a tea blender has sufficient access to a consistent supply of ingredients, they can start the daunting task of tasting, ensuring each ingredient conforms to their high standards. There is no automated process or machine that can accurately taste and determine whether the ingredient or blend conforms. Only a well trained nose and tongue can give accurate results.

Keep in mind that blenders need to track and taste every production of each ingredient in their assortment. Let's say they receive an ingredient shipment ten times per year. Apply that to their inventory of 1,000 ingredients and then assume the ingredient is used in 100 different blends. It is not hard to see the mounting complexity. As a talented tea-taster himself, Max's take is:

This is the primary job of a tea taster, to make sure that there is consistency in tea batches. Natural changes are going to occur and those can't be helped. But it's the job of the tea taster to look at the product and decide if the changes are so small that the consumer won't detect it.

If we think that the change is going to be really noticeable, then we have to be flexible with the ingredients we are using. We may have to change the flavor profile or the origin of some of the ingredients. There are times when you have to tell the customer that you are not able to hold the same standard as you did a few years ago, so we have to make an adjustment.

Tea blenders should proactively make small changes to maintain a blend's flavor profile from batch to batch if needed. This is usually done by altering the composition of the ingredients slightly or swapping ingredients to different origins.

A great example of this is with apple pieces. Turkey is one of the largest suppliers of dried apples that tend to have a mild, sweet taste. Blenders also buy apples from Eastern Europe which tend to be more sour. If the Eastern European apples are slightly more sour one year, the blender might include some Turkish apples in blends to curb the acidity and keep the blend balanced.

The same rigor is used to maintain the visual appearance when evaluating large cut ingredients for use in loose leaf tea blends. Stunning visuals can help amplify the aromas and tastes in the mind of the consumer.

These changes are not made to confuse consumers or keep information hidden. Instead, the changes provide consumers with a tasty, attractive product that meets their expectations over the course of many years. Taste is the main driver for purchases of consumable products, so maintaining consistency is vital.

Bear in mind that as much as humanly possible, decisions in maintaining taste profiles are made objectively. A tea blender may not personally enjoy a certain product, but they need to act on behalf of their customer. Remember what I said at the start of the book? There is no bad tea.

Most specialty tea companies are brands that focus on marketing and distribution. They are in front of the end consumer daily; but they rely on their tea blending partners to deliver a consistent product that meets their customer's demands.

Max said:

I think that the key to a successful partnership is for a company to be transparent with their customers and communicate well. From our point of view, we are just the importer and blender of the products. We don't know who the end consumer is who will drink the tea.

CONSISTENCY IN COST

Arguably, one of the most difficult variables to keep consistent is cost. Nevertheless, it is one of the most important factors for a tea blender to consider. There are many hidden reasons behind the cost of a blended tea. The most significant of which is the final retail price. A brand ultimately decides what price to charge consumers. For the purposes of this chapter, I will focus instead on the factors that contribute to the prices set by a large tea supplier.

How the Ingredient Is Sourced

First and foremost, a supplier needs to purchase ingredients. They negotiate with gardens to get the best price. Committing to long-term purchasing contracts or buying significant amounts of ingredients may lead to price reduction. Like many other industries, buying larger volumes of products can significantly reduce unit costs.

Size Of the Ingredient

It is folly to believe that the smaller the ingredient cut is, the cheaper it will be. The primary determining factor is whether the ingredient needs extra processing to get to a smaller size.

Certain ingredients, such as black tea, are sifted during processing with no further steps necessary to make the ingredient smaller. In this case, smaller cut sizes of black teas are usually less expensive. This is not the case across the board, however. If ingredients need to be manually cut or in some way altered, this will add to the cost.

Shipping

Shipping costs have a significant impact on price. Tea blenders source from many countries, and the more they can consolidate their purchases, the better. The volume and the urgent need for a given product will determine whether it is shipped by land, sea or air, and if insurance is needed for the shipment. Customs charges in each country also add to the overall shipping cost.

Ingredient Testing

Tea is a food product, so ingredients need to be tested in labs for safety and to comply with regulations in each country. Lab tests will determine if an ingredient is contaminated with bacteria, fungi or other microbes. Testing will also determine if pesticides, herbicides and heavy metals are above set limits.

To ensure a completely safe product for their customers, the suppliers take spot tests and multiple samples from each batch of ingredients that arrives at their warehouse.

Cleaning The Materials

Suppliers may choose to clean certain ingredients in addition to performing lab tests. Cleaning a product could be as simple as having employees sift through to pick out any debris, or as complex as treating them with steam, ultraviolet light, or carbon dioxide.

There are also cleaning procedures to sanitize the

Flavoring

Flavoring is probably one of the most surprising cost drivers in the blended tea industry. On average, it is the most expensive raw material used in tea blends, even though it is used in lower percentages than other ingredients. Flavors come in an array of types, all with varying degrees of cost. It is also a volatile material that needs special storage conditions, adding further cost for the tea blender.

Packaging Formats

Each customer has specific requirements for how they want their tea packed, and every option has a different cost. Each packaging option offered by a supplier will impact the final price, from boxes of 20 tea bags to 20 kilogram sacks.

Costs Vary

It might seem redundant, but the truth is that every cost factor listed above is subject to change at a moment's notice. This does not even account for economic factors such as inflation. Simply put, no cost is entirely stable. Tea blenders need to account for changes and balance costs where they can to keep their customers satisfied.

blending equipment to ensure there is no cross-contamination of different tastes and allergens between each batch. These are all part of normal food manufacturing processes but do add to the supplier's overhead.

Ingredient Turnover

A company has better costs on an ingredient that moves through its warehouse quickly. Apple pieces, for example, are included in many blended teas, so a supplier sells that inventory rapidly.

On the other hand, they may have a large cut, dried yuzu peel that has a lower demand. Usually, this item will cost more since it takes up space in their warehouse for a longer time period.

Certifications

Tea manufacturers need some level of food sa[fety] certification, especially to sell in certain ma[rkets]. If they want to carry organic, kosher, or ot[her] auxiliary product certifications, these wil[l add] costs to the supplier. These prices will c[hange] based on the bureaucracy of the organ[ization] that handle each certification.

Now that we have gone over the complexities of the supply chain, you should have a better understanding of what goes on behind the scenes of the tea you purchase. This information should also prove helpful for a brand trying to choose a good supplier.

SUPPLIERS AS PARTNERS

Brands that view their suppliers as extensions of their own teams tend to have the healthiest relationships. Since many tea blends are developed for long-term sales, a brand will likely need to rely on a supplier for long-term consistency of their tea product line. This allows brands to focus on what they do best–marketing and distribution.

Brands should give plenty of thought into securing a solid partner, or partners, for their tea business. There are plenty of ways to find reputable tea blenders:

- Referrals from others in the business
- Tea industry networking events
- Industry publications
- Trade shows
- Tea event sponsors
- Internet searches

In my experience, getting introductions to blending partners through referrals leads to great relationships. Regardless of how a brand finds a manufacturer, it is important that they partner with one that is adaptable and transparent about product shifts where necessary.

RED FLAGS

Brands should not change suppliers frequently, but there may be times when they need to find an alternative blending partner. The biggest red flag to watch for is inconsistency.

Inconsistencies can happen for all the reasons stated above: inventory, taste, and cost. Humans are still human, and mistakes will happen. But if it is happening too often without reasonable explanations, it may be time for a brand to move on.

If a brand knows the formula for their tea blend, which is unlikely, they can try to take the formula elsewhere. Even if a brand knows the percentages of the ingredients, most tea blenders do not disclose the flavoring component. This is sometimes seen as their "secret sauce" that differentiates them among other suppliers.

In the absence of knowing the full recipe, good tea blenders can use a sample of tea to recreate a blend. It is possible to blend a tea that is close enough in flavor, even without knowing the precise flavorings used.

I want you to know that we are just scratching the surface of the tea supply chain in this book. What I hope you take away is that a reputable supplier, regardless of the complexities, should be informative of their supply chain shifts. They should be transparent about where their ingredients come from, and brands should ask for the information.

Each supplier has its own specialities and niche market segments, so a brand should consider multiple variables before choosing the right blending partner.

The good news about the tea industry is that no matter how big or how small any brand is, there is a manufacturing partner out there that is right for them.

4

ANATOMY OF A TEA BLEND

Imagine you are tasting a tea blend called "Strawberry Delight" and notice the ingredient list has black tea, freeze-dried strawberry, flavor, and pink cornflower petals. This is a simple and typical example that you might find in a tea retailer's assortment. You look over the ingredients and think, *Wow, the addition of the strawberry pieces really brings out that ripe strawberry note, and the flower petals are beautiful!*

Most labels do not disclose the weight percentage of each ingredient, so let me pull back that curtain for you. It might be that 92% of the blend is made up of black tea, only 5% is freeze-dried strawberries, 2% is flavor, and 1% is pink cornflower petals. That does not seem like enough strawberry to bring out such a potent flavor, does it?

Truth be told, the only components of this blend that you actually taste are the black tea and the flavoring. The black tea absorbs and carries the flavoring that mimics the taste of strawberry, not the strawberries themselves. If this shocks you, you are not alone!

However, a blender's first instinct is to add strawberry pieces because it gives the brain a visual cue to recognize the strawberry as the dominant flavor. This is part of the magic, mystery, and wonder of the blended tea world. Every ingredient in the blend has a purpose, just not the one you may think.

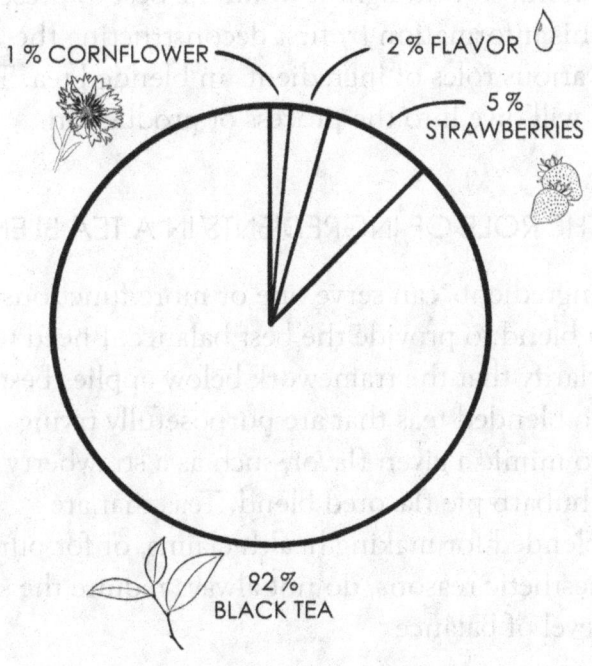

I will not be systematically answering questions in this chapter, but it did need to be included because customers and tea industry professionals submitted questions to me about where and how teas are blended. A few common questions were:

1. Where was the tea blended?
2. How does a company flavor tea?
3. Was the tea blended in house?
4. How is a tea blend created?

These questions are going to be specific to each brand, so I thought it would be best to present this information by first deconstructing the various roles of ingredients in blended tea. Then I will dive into the process of production.

THE ROLE OF INGREDIENTS IN A TEA BLEND

Ingredients can serve one or more functions in a blend to provide the best balance. I need to clarify that the framework below applies best to blended teas that are purposefully trying to mimic a given flavor, such as a strawberry rhubarb pie flavored blend. Teas that are blended for making health claims, or for purely aesthetic reasons, do not always require the same level of balance.

1. Flavor Carriers

Certain ingredients are considered flavor carriers. Liquid flavor is best applied on a tea blend that can absorb and retain the flavor until it is steeped in hot water. The ingredients release the flavor into the water as the tea is steeped. If a blend has solid flavor capsules, they will need to be suspended properly in a tea blend so that each cup has the same amount. Just like a bag of chips, smaller particles settle to the bottom with time and movement, and a blender needs to add ingredients that will keep the flavor capsules suspended so that each cup has the same amount of flavor.

Examples of flavor carrier ingredients include apple, camellia sinensis and rooibos. These ingredients absorb added moisture in the form of liquid flavoring. Other fruits, herbs and botanicals can be added to a blend, but any added flavoring dispersed into the cup by flavor carriers will likely be the most prominent flavor in the cup.

2. Mouthfeel and Body

A tea blend needs to steep a cup of tea with mouthfeel and body. What does that mean?

Have you ever had hot chocolate, powdered drink mix, or iced coffee that tastes watered-down or thin? It does not make for a great tasting experience, so we want to avoid that.

Certain ingredients in the tea blend will lend body and mouthfeel to the tea so that it does not seem watered down. These ingredients include camellia sinensis, hibiscus, chicory root, rooibos, and licorice root. In addition to mouthfeel and body, ingredients also bring their own flavors, so a blender needs to choose the right ingredients to balance the tastes. For example, they may want to add hibiscus for a thick mouthfeel, but too much will make the blend extremely tart.

3. The Five Basic Tastes

Our tongues experience five basic tastes: sweet, sour, salty, bitter, and umami. In blended tea, the most common tastes you will experience are sweet, sour, and bitter. There are rare instances where you may find salty and umami, such as a salted caramel tea blend.

Just as in cooking, there needs to be a balance of these essential tastes to create something that is pleasurable. A blender does not want to make a tea that is overly bitter or too sour. Balancing the flavors is key, or they will create a tea blend that is not sellable. It is good to stretch creative liberties for certain flavor profiles and bend this rule from time to time. If a blender's task is to make a sour cherry flavored tea blend, they should probably bring more sourness to that cup than for other cherry blends.

Some of the ingredients that are used to balance the five tastes include: camellia sinensis for bitterness, sweet blackberry leaf and licorice root for sweetness, and hibiscus and apple pomace for sourness. There are hundreds of fruits, herbs and botanicals to choose from, so it is a good practice to constantly taste ingredients on their own to determine what taste they will lend to the cup.

4. Aromatic Complexity

Generally speaking, ingredients that give aromatic complexity are spices and potent herbs. The difference in these ingredients is that they do not drastically alter the five basic tastes or overall mouthfeel of the blend. These ingredients complement and enhance the desired cup profile.

If a blender is aiming for a strawberry flavored tea, they will likely use a combination of different flavorings to achieve it. However, maybe it is missing a brightness in the aroma which would otherwise evoke a fresh berry flavor. The blender might choose to add some lemongrass, which has a naturally bright, citrus aroma, to enhance the fresh strawberry note.

Ingredients commonly used to add aromatic complexity include lemongrass, ginger, and mint. This list barely scratches the surface. Again, taste as many ingredients as you can, as often as possible. That is the best way to know how they will impact the final cup.

5. Visual Interest

Tea blends, especially loose leaf blends, can be visually stunning. The appearance of a tea blend can make the flavor and aroma more appealing and give consumers a visual cue to identify the flavor direction of the blend. Our example at the beginning of this chapter was adding freeze dried strawberry pieces to tangibly lead the customer to taste strawberry. This practice can be applied to all manner of fruits, confections, or any other flavor a brand wants to mimic. Caramel pieces added to a caramel flavored blend, or almond slices to a marzipan flavored blend, the examples are endless.

There are three components to visual interest:

- Visual interest in the dry leaf
- Visual interest in the cup color
- Visual interest in the ingredients for a marketing purpose

Usually, the goal is to make a tea blend that looks appealing in the package and when it steeps. Some ingredients are added to heighten the visual appeal of a tea blend, usually flowers or large slices of fruit. Ingredients can also alter the tea's color in the cup. For instance, steeped beetroot results in a beautiful pink color when used in small quantities. A popular ingredient in tea blending recently is butterfly pea flower which steeps a deep blue hue.

Another thing to consider is the ingredient list on a tea package. If a customer buys a strawberry flavored tea and does not see strawberries in the blend, that could be a problem. Most consumers are going to expect to see ingredients in the blend that they associate with the flavor they purchased.

This is also common in tea blends that are marketed to a more health conscious consumer.

Valerian root is traditionally used as a sleep aid, but in my opinion, it smells and tastes like dirty socks. A blender probably does not want a blend to taste like valerian root, but adding a small amount cues the customer to identify the blend as a possible sleep aid.

6. Cost Containment

Each ingredient in a tea blend has a specific cost to the supplier. The percentage of each ingredient will have an impact on the overall cost of the blend. Many factors go into the price of each ingredient, and those costs change from year to year. There is more information on how ingredients are priced in the preceding chapter.

Tea suppliers will not be keen to share their individual ingredient costs with their customers, but customers should be up front about their cost restrictions and price targets. Communication is key here, and there are options to suit every budget. Be aware that added flavorings are usually the most expensive ingredients to a blender.

A good tea supplier will work with their customers to provide cost-effective blends. This is why tea blends can include so many other ingredients aside from the marketed flavor. Some ingredients are there to balance overall costs.

WHAT MAKES A GOOD TEA BLEND?

A good tea blend needs to have the right flavor profile for its target market and have the appropriate flavors balanced, all at an acceptable price point.

You have likely never heard of woodruff if you are from North America. If a woodruff flavored tea blend was sold at a typical grocery store, chances are you would not buy it. However, this is a popular flavor for confections and beverages in Germany, so that market is more likely to buy a woodruff tea.

This regional difference in flavors even extends to more common foods. For instance, the cherry flavor preferred in Europe is more tart and sharp tasting, while in North America, the market usually likes cherry flavoring to be sweet and juicy.

Brands should be open with their suppliers on their intended target markets, as they may have insights into which flavors perform better in different regions. A brand should also feel comfortable giving guidance on specific flavor attributes they may want altered in a blend. If they learn that their customers do not like a certain strawberry flavoring, the blender should be able to either offer a new product or tweak the flavor in that tea.

I spoke to Maximillian Frick, a general manager and tea taster at Mount Everest Tea. He shared some useful information about the supply chain of blended tea, which is covered in the preceding chapter. He also walked me through the process of creating a custom tea blend for a brand, which is captured below.

Before diving into the process of developing a custom tea blend, a brand should first ask to taste samples of current blends a vendor has in their assortment, usually referred to as their catalog. This will give an overview of the various flavors, ingredients, and straight teas a vendor carries.

A brand might find their perfect product assortment in these pre-developed blends. The benefit of sourcing through a vendor's catalog is that the blends are price competitive since they are usually buying large volumes of those ingredients. The brand might not have to commit to buying large volumes of ingredients and thus be stuck with inventory. Once a brand truly decides that nothing in the vendor's assortment is appropriate, then they should open the conversation of developing custom blends.

CUSTOM BLENDS

Custom blend development is no easy task. A brand not only needs to determine their ideal assortment of flavors and workable price points but also respond to a number of inquiries from their partner blender. The goal of this section is to help brands better understand the information a development partner may ask so they are aware of the complexities.

The first question is whether a brand wants to closely match a certain tea blend currently on the market, or if they want blends from scratch. If the brand does want to match specific flavors of commercially available blends, then they would submit these to their partner blender and have them try to match them as closely as possible. A blender can usually come close, if not identical, to matching blends in tastes, visuals, and prices.

The process is more involved if the brand decides they want to create blends from scratch. Max walked me through a few examples of initial questions they would ask clients looking for custom blends:

1. What flavor profile are the blends? Are there any specific ingredients to use?
2. What quantity of each blend do they need to purchase?
3. What certifications do they want? Example: organic?
4. What are the price targets?
5. In what country, or countries, will the blends be sold?
6. What are the food and beverage regulations of the country, or countries?
7. How often will the blend, or blends, need to be shipped?
8. In what packaging format do the blends need to be shipped? Example: tea bags, or one kilogram bags.

Tea vendors need this level of detail due to the complexity of their supply chain, which is discussed in a different chapter. It is their job to assimilate all the information the customer provides and deliver salable blends at the right price. There will be instances that a request might prove difficult to fulfill, but a supplier should be informative of any obstacles and ready to provide alternatives.

Let us imagine that a tea brand wants a supplier to source a special rose blossom from Saudi Arabia for a tea blend. The supplier investigates but learns that this blossom only grows once a year, and the production yields inconsistent quantities. They have the option to buy these blossoms for the client but determine it to be risky as it could jeopardize the long term consistency of the blend.

The supplier should clearly communicate any challenges and suggest alternatives to use in blends, as it is the primary responsibility of the tea blender to maintain a blend's consistency. In the case of the special rose blossoms, a supplier could suggest a different blossom. If the client is adamant they use the special blossoms, a supplier might advise blending in some other rose blossoms to reduce the quantity of special ones needed.

Tea blenders might go through several blend iterations before a client is satisfied with the taste, cost, and visual of a product. This process can be accelerated with more detailed communication. It is helpful to a supplier if a client is specific as to how a product needs to be altered.

They might say to their supplier, *This blend is too expensive*. But this direction is unclear. It would be better to communicate a specific cost target the supplier can use as guidance. Similarly, saying, *use a sweeter strawberry flavor* is more descriptive than, *this is the wrong strawberry flavor*.

In the end, the key to developing tea blends is communication. Creating a beneficial relationship with a blending partner is paramount to a brand's success. A good partner blender cares about the success of their clients since the growth is mutually beneficial.

LARGE SCALE BLENDING PROCESS

Once a blend is finalized and ordered by a client, the blender needs to produce the necessary quantity. The first thing for a blender to consider is whether or not all of the raw materials are available, or whether they will need to source additional quantities on the client's behalf.

Then, the order needs to be scheduled into their production plan.

There are many sizes and types of tea blending machines available, but they all perform the same task; mixing the individual ingredients into a homogenous blend while retaining their integrity. There is a common misconception that all the ingredients in a blend are thrown together all at once and mixed. It is not that easy.

A blender will establish a blending recipe for the larger production, which will determine when ingredients are added in to the machine. Lighter, more fragile ingredients are normally added last to avoid crushing them. If, for example, they add whole rosebuds into the machine too early, the mixing process could crush them into powder, and they might have to discard the whole lot. A successful blending process ends with a homogenous product that will taste the same from one cup to the next.

After the blending is complete, the vendor packages it according to the client's needs. Some blending companies offer different packaging options and could be a brand's one-stop shop for a finished branded product. A brand can have a custom blended product manufactured and packaged into tea bags all under one roof.

CAN A TEA BRAND BLEND ITS OWN TEA?

I have so far been focusing on large blending companies which focus on manufacturing for different brands. Can individual tea brands blend teas for themselves? Yes, tea brands can blend for themselves. However, I have seen too many examples of brands that have not thought through the implications.

Tea is considered a food product according to most government standards, so a company needs to be in compliance with their local health and safety laws. Brands should be aware of all necessary documents and certifications needed to manufacture food in their region. I have seen too many cases where this is overlooked, and it can have dire consequences.

Brands need to consider their core competencies before diving into the world of blending on their own. Managing product consistency in inventory, taste, and cost poses challenges and could detract from marketing and distribution efforts. A brand needs to put generous resources behind the blending operation, no matter the scale. This is something I can personally attest to.

I attended a small university in Anderson, Indiana, where I had the fortune of meeting a fellow student who was equally passionate about tea. I was a hobbyist and blogger at the time, but he had taken his passion further and started a tea business from his dorm room, BourgeaTEA. I shadowed him and ended up purchasing the company before he graduated. I had become a business student operating a small business right after completing my first year of studies. It was a tremendous opportunity to test my entrepreneurial drive.

The tea blends were marketed as custom blended, but that was only half the truth. I quickly learned that sourcing flavoring and various ingredients was a messy endeavor, especially when my main focus needed to be sales and marketing. The teas purchased were already blended with flavoring, and I would mix dried fruit, other botanicals, or even multi-colored sprinkles into the teas and package them by hand. I would individually portion blends into tea bags and seal them with a hot straightening iron. It was monotonous work for a business student.

My predecessor had already researched local food safety laws and had received a health certificate by performing blending in a certified shared kitchen. Truth be told, I never blended tea in that shared kitchen. I followed as many common sense health rules as I could think of, including wearing gloves and a mask, and sanitizing equipment post-blending, but it was probably not legal in retrospect.

The tea business was eventually purchased by a coffee company, which I helped found. This helped increase tea sales, and I quickly realized blending and packing by hand was not sustainable. I called around to a few tea suppliers and eventually got connected with one that was nearby, which was surprising considering we were in rural Indiana. The first step was matching existing tea blends, which was partially successful. It was my first experience developing unique blends alongside an established tea blender. The first custom blend was a mix of rooibos, honeybush, linden leaf, and natural vanilla flavoring. The blend went on to be the second highest selling blend for our budding business.

If I could go back in time, the first thing I would do is locate a trustworthy blending partner. I would then have more time to devote to marketing, sales and distribution efforts. My assumption was that no company would want to supply a small business like mine, but that was simply not true. A brand, regardless of their unique identity, can find a blending partner to suit their needs.

CONSIDERATIONS OF BLENDED TEA

Drinking blended tea is a multi-sensory experience. Customers interact with the visual, aroma and taste. All ingredients in blended tea serve a purpose, and it is not always obvious what that purpose is. Brands need to focus on marketing blends that meet their customers' taste expectations, brand perceptions, and price point.

Brands should work in harmony with their suppliers to source products that will sell to their intended audience. Clear and detailed communication is necessary between a brand and their supplier, whether they are related to catalog tea blends or custom formulations. If brands have a solid understanding of why certain ingredients are used, they will be able to better direct suppliers to meet their customers' needs.

If a brand decides to manufacture their own blends, they need to be aware of the implications from logistics and inventory management, to food safety and local health laws. A brand should take this on only if they have sufficient resources to support it without detracting from other core competencies.

Tea blending is a lifelong learning experience and a creative outlet unlike any other. I encourage anyone in the tea industry to learn and appreciate the nuances, challenges and complexities of blending.

5
CERTIFICATIONS AND OTHER LABELS

Do you want to sell teas that are organic, fair trade, kosher, or vegan? There is much to consider when making those designations. The first thing to answer is whether or not having a certification is necessary.

Consumers have a myriad of questions about the products they buy. Whether for ethical reasons, dietary needs, or religious reasons, certifications from organizations across the world give consumers confidence that products align with their personal values or consumption needs.

Before we address this topic, I need to mention that I will not be exploring the politics of certifications, or providing my opinions on the ethics of certifying agencies. I will, however, cover how certifications relate to the tea industry, with a focus on leveraging them for marketing purposes. I use the term "certifications" or "certified products" as an umbrella term encompassing a number of possible labels a company could have on its product. Each has its benefits and complexities, but I will not address them all individually.

I debated whether or not to include a chapter on certifications due to the heated opinions, differing politics, and personal emotions tied to them. Ultimately, I realized that excluding this chapter would be a disservice since there were many questions submitted about them in my initial survey of my industry colleagues.

I urge you to read this chapter objectively. How you personally feel about certifications is not relevant. What matters for a tea brand is whether certifications address the needs of their consumers and theoretically lead to increased sales.

There are challenges in obtaining and maintaining third party certifications. Many companies choose not to have their products certified, even if they meet the requirements. The primary pragmatic reason a brand should consider getting third party certifications is if certification will lead to increased sales.

To gain an applicable perspective on certifications and their role in a tea business, I spoke with Don Ho, a tea entrepreneur and consultant. He founded a company called Harmony Tea Bar in Orange County, California. Harmony Tea Bar was established as a premium, quick service tea bar focused on natural and organic products. Don learned firsthand the benefits and drawbacks of integrating certified products at the core of a tea business.

MEETING CUSTOMER EXPECTATIONS

The first, and probably most important consideration before deciding to sell certified products is whether or not the target market values them. Harmony Tea Bar is based in Orange County, California, where there is a large market of affluent and health conscious customers. They are more prone to seek out organic certified products; so integrating organic products into the core of the business was deemed essential.

However, if a tea brand's clientele is less affluent, or in a region with different values, the average consumers might not be willing to pay the premiums associated with certified products. It is no secret that products with special certifications generally tend to be more expensive. A brand needs to know that their customers will pay the premium. There is a conception that products with certifications are of higher quality and will taste better; but this is not necessarily true. The higher cost is due in part to the administrative and operational work associated with the organizations or agencies maintaining the integrity of those certifications.

Certifications do not necessarily carry the same importance in different regions. For example, North American and European consumers tend to value certain claims more than general consumers in Asia. Organic products, for instance, might be too costly for consumers in Asia, and the market does not value the certifications in the same way. It may not be worth it for a brand to go through the process of sourcing and maintaining certified products because it may not result in higher sales in that region.

THE CHALLENGES OF CERTIFIED PRODUCTS

Brands need to anticipate challenges if they decide that integrating certified teas into their catalog is the right move. Recall that maintaining product consistency over time is one of the most important factors for developing a client base. Sourcing certified products adds extra layers of complexity to maintaining consistency in the three key areas in the supply chain: inventory, taste, and cost.

Matcha, a powdered green tea from Japan, provides a good example to illustrate how certification impacts sourcing consistency. Matcha is produced at scale in Japan, China and Korea, and organic and non-organic options are available.

Japan is globally recognized as the leader in manufacturing high quality matcha. However, the Japanese market does not value organic certified products in the same way that North American or European consumers do. Historically, the agricultural industry in Japan did not invest in transitioning or creating more certified organic tea gardens for matcha production.

Therefore, this led to a greater demand for organic matcha but less overall supply. China stepped in to fill the void, and now they are a major producer of organic matcha. However, many consumers prefer the taste of Japanese matcha but ideally want it certified organic. Japanese matcha tends to be sweeter and smoother, with a more vibrant green color. This has resulted in a low supply of organic Japanese matcha while the cost has dramatically risen.

At Harmony Tea Bar, having organic products was core to the brand identity. But we always told our customers that the number one priority was having the best tasting products. We decided that organic matcha did not deliver the best taste for our customers, so instead, we sourced high quality, non-organic matcha from Japan, said Don. *We found other incredible organic teas to offer to our customers, though, so we were still able to fulfill our brand promise.*

Most certifying agencies require growers to pay for their certifications, but this does not guarantee that they will be able to sell their product at a premium. Not all growers will take this risk, even if their field or factory is eligible to be certified. The result is that there are a limited number of certified products available globally. I alluded to this in the chapter about flavoring as well. The limitations in sourcing ingredients are among the reasons companies may rely on artificial flavoring. The same concept applies to sourcing organic products.

There was a time when there was a global shortage of organic cornflower petals. It is a common ingredient in blending, but is normally used in small percentages as a visual component. DAVIDsTEA had to work with their suppliers and the agencies that certified their tea blends to find a solution to keep their organic status. Each country and agency has different rules regarding organic products and labeling. Eventually, a solution was found, but it took a great deal of time and resources.

Harmony Tea Bar had a fantastic, organic Thai iced tea, but it was a while before it made it onto the menu. Thai iced tea is a bold black tea with a combination of spices, flavoring and dye that, when steeped and mixed with sweetened condensed milk, creates a vibrant orange, creamy, flavor packed beverage. The flavors and colors added to Thai iced tea are almost universally artificial and difficult to replicate naturally.

That's actually one of the big successes at Harmony Tea Bar that I like to talk about, said Don. *I worked with one of my vendors for ten months to develop that tea blend. We went back and forth about twelve times before I was satisfied with it. But it became our top selling drink by far. All the other tea shops in the region sold Thai iced tea, but ours was the only one that was fully organic, with no artificial flavors or colors.*

Brands that decide to include certified products in their portfolio will undoubtedly have issues maintaining consistency in their inventories, tastes, and costs. But partnering with reputable tea blenders and suppliers can ease some of this complexity and help deliver certified products that meet their customers' needs.

THE HIDDEN COSTS OF CERTIFICATIONS

There is a common misconception that certified products cost more because the ingredients are of a higher quality. It is common to think that the premiums consumers pay on those products go back to the producers, factories and workers, but this is not always the case. Certifying agencies, nonprofits, and not-for-profit organizations need operational revenue.

The high level structure of organic certification

CERTIFICATIONS AND OTHER LABELS

provides a good example. The certifying agencies drive revenue through dues paid by farms that adhere to organic growing standards. The farms benefit from being able to market their products as certified organic, but need to charge more for their products to compensate. The farms also need to comply with strict regulations for pesticide usage and soil management which could potentially lead to lower yields.

This premium is passed on to consumers in the final price, with the money distributed through the entire supply chain, and to the certifying agency. Some certifying agencies also receive government funding and facilitate grants to offset costs for producers to transition to organic. So there is some distribution down the chain.

In my experience, it is not uncommon to meet small scale tea growers that adhere to organic growing standards but cannot afford, or would not benefit monetarily, from being certified as organic. In one particular instance in Taiwan, I met a small grower who said that being certified organic was not good enough, and set even more strict growing practices for their own garden.

I would urge consumers and businesses alike

to do their research and understand the organizational structure and the money trail of the certifications they value. The pursuit of more information will help further the accountability of the certifying agencies, so they can carry out their missions to benefit people, the planet, and the products.

PURSUING CERTIFICATIONS

I wanted to cover all of this information not to discourage brands from pursuing certified products or encourage consumers to change their values. I hope what comes from this is a yearning to learn more, and for brands to be armed with information that will help foster mutually beneficial conversations with their partner suppliers.

Before pursuing certified products, several questions tea brands should ask themselves are:

- Will the brand be able to leverage this certification in marketing efforts and increase sales?
- Is it possible to create certified tea products that satisfy the preferred flavor profiles of the target customers?

- Will the target customers pay the premium on the certified products, thereby providing a healthy profit margin for the brand?

Brands must anticipate and be prepared for challenges in their supply chain if they decide that certified products are vital. There are tea suppliers that specialize in providing products with specific certifications, and a brand should seek these out as their partner suppliers.

LABELING FOOD PRODUCTS

Blended tea is considered a food product, so brands need to follow strict rules and guidelines set by the certifying agencies. These encompass everything from how products are labeled for import and export, to how the certifying agencies need to be referenced in marketing material. There are even strict size, color, and placement guidelines that brands must follow for using their logos and badges.

Many tea blending companies have departments dedicated to managing certifications. Some may extend this knowledge to their clients, providing resources and instructions to help brands maintain their own certifications.

However, not all certifications are recognized in every country. There may be instances where a brand will need to direct their suppliers regarding specific needs in order to maintain certification in their local market. This requires a great deal of research, and some brands have entire departments dedicated to this.

For example, not all countries have the same requirements for declaring allergies on packaged food products. It is not uncommon for tea blends to contain ingredients like nuts, dairy, or soy, which can trigger severe allergic reactions. Some countries have strict laws dictating what allergies need to be declared on packages. Reputable tea suppliers have all this information available, but brands might need to ask for more depending on where they want to sell their product.

MAKE A GOOD BUSINESS DECISION

Tea companies cannot exist without profit. They can be tea advocates, deeply passionate and willing to share their excitement with the world, but when it comes down to it, they need sustained sales to operate. Companies need to understand who their customer is, the values of

CERTIFICATIONS AND OTHER LABELS

their customer, and whether or not investing in certifications will increase their sales, all while keeping in mind that a brand can source ethical and environmentally friendly products without carrying a badge of certification to prove it. But certifications can be an easy way to authenticate those stories with consumers.

Education is key, and brands should leverage the knowledge of their suppliers to determine what is feasible and appropriate for them. That is why it is important for brands to partner with blenders that are transparent in all regards. The tea blender can help guide a brand and co-create products that resonate with the values of their customers and meet their flavor expectations.

6
ANECDOTES FROM THE TEA INDUSTRY

There is so much information necessary to outline the processes of blended and flavored tea. The truth is, each chapter here could be its own book. I deliberately kept the information as concise as I could and tried to focus my efforts on the most important elements. The purpose of this text was to answer the most immediate questions in an easily digestible manner.

I entered the tea industry and was entranced by the ever-present spirit of community. There are many people who helped me get to where I am today, and my goal is to support the ambitions of others who share this passion.

Arnaud Petitvallet and his business partner, Max Rivest, set out to create a brand new tea product in 2014. They have since won awards with their innovative product, a tea made from coffee leaves, and continue to grow. During a casual conversation with Arnaud, I shared my goal of writing this book and asked if they would have used a resource like this in their early stages.

Of course I would, he said. *It is a no-brainer. I had no clue what I was doing when I started down this path, and I had no understanding of the tea industry. I do not think anybody has written about how the tea industry functions, or how it works from production to final resale.*

What I learned on my journey is that it is very compartmentalized. People in the tea shop will know that they buy from this one manufacturer, but they do not know anything else about the process. There are no direct connections in the supply chain, and there are so many middlemen that it is even more confusing. It is rare that someone in the tea industry would know the entire extent.

Arnaud and Max had many challenges when they were creating their new product. Arnaud said that if they had a resource like this early on, they probably could have shortened their time to commercialization by years. They needed the right introductions to other people in the industry in order to fill the void of information about the tea supply chain.

It does not matter whether you are passionate about straight tea, blended tea, or both; you can find common ground in the shared love of tea throughout the industry. Kevin Gascoyne, one of the founders of Camellia Sinensis, which specializes in straight tea said:

Single-origin teas would not have developed in recent years to where they are today without flavored teas. They have had a symbiotic series of developmental steps.

Blended tea and straight tea both support the industry and continue to inspire innovations in the tea category overall. The differentiating factor is the addition, or exclusion, of flavoring. I believe flavoring has a permanent place in the story of tea and is beneficial to its future growth. This is why there is a chapter solely dedicated to it.

Consumers value the taste of the food and beverage items they purchase. For some consumers, that means an artisanal, single-origin tea; for others, it means a familiar flavor that provides an anchor to an otherwise unknown product. It is vital that brands align their flavor offerings to meet their target market's needs. The final product might taste great to the brand owner, but if it does not sell, it is time to re-evaluate.

Marzi Pecen, a tea and sensory consultant, told me a story pertaining to regional differences in flavorings that I thought was an appropriate example.

A friend of mine was making an iced tea blend for a restaurant, and they requested that it be yuzu flavored. She did not have that flavor in-house, but the restaurant wanted it fast. To meet their request, she mixed two different citrus flavors to create a taste similar enough to yuzu. In this specific market, that solution was fine. However, this would not have worked if she had been creating the flavor for a Japanese client or a fine dining establishment.

As mentioned in the flavoring section, there are ingredients that can be used, both artificial and natural, to mimic various flavor profiles. The most important thing about creating a blended tea is that it matches the palate expectations of the consumer.

Some people, even those inside the tea industry,

consider flavored tea to be a simple matter: mix some tea or herbs with flavoring, and voila, a flavored tea is made. Contrary to that belief, creating a well composed blended tea is a complicated task.

People do not realize what it takes to create a stable, consistent product that is going to taste like you want it to and expect it to. Given that tea changes from year to year, harvest to harvest, and location to location, it is miraculous that it has any sense of consistency, said Marzi.

She is absolutely right. A tea company's biggest challenge is to find a blending partner that provides consistent products year after year. The good news is that no matter what a company's needs are, there is a blender out there that is the right partner for them. The challenge is finding those partners. While speaking with Arnaud, he shared his struggles with finding the right partners to develop their product line.

In this industry, unless you know someone who can make a tea blend for you, you are out of luck. When we started our product development, we went with basic blends and added in a few types of ingredients we were aware of. We just had to look at the types of teas people were drinking and what it was mixed with, and go from there.

The way we were blending tea was rudimentary because of the initial co-packer we were working with. We were limited by what they provided. Eventually, we moved to a different co-packer that we found through word of mouth. This company helped us expand the type of ingredients we could add to our tea blends. It was revolutionary to me because I had no idea you could add certain ingredients. Making the change to the right co-packer allowed us to develop a real tea product that got us started down the path to where we are now. There was just no information about any of this. Finding blenders and co-packers was difficult because you have to know someone who knows them.

Everything Arnaud experienced is still an issue in the tea industry. It is vital to know someone with insider knowledge to help navigate the supply chain and find suppliers. In chapter four, I go into more detail about the processes behind developing tea blends with suppliers. I also cover the pros and cons of creating a custom blend. Many companies will actually choose to resell tea blends from a supplier's blend catalog.

Before a brand gets to the point where they choose a supplier, they will need to understand a bit about ingredient compositions. This understanding provides a foundation of knowledge that is helpful when discussing blends with suppliers. Communication with suppliers will be more effective when additional research is done in advance. Ultimately, educating yourself will help you as a brand to more quickly achieve what you are seeking.

When speaking to Don Ho, a tea entrepreneur and consultant, he mentioned that one of his biggest success stories was creating an organic Thai tea blend. He knew the right language to use with his supplier and was able to steer them in the right direction quickly.

When we developed our brand's mission statement, we promised customers that we were never going to sell them anything with artificial flavors, colors, ingredients, or high fructose corn syrup. Unfortunately, I did not fully understand that brand promise when we got started and it came back to bite us. We found ways to work around it but it made things harder in terms of sourcing items and not being able to produce popular drinks our customers expected.

However, one of our big successes was creating an organic Thai tea. Thai teas usually have several artificial colors added. I worked with one of my vendors to create this blend. It took us twelve different versions before we finally nailed down the finished product. It actually turned into one of our best-selling drinks once we were able to explain to our customers why it was so special.

The main takeaway from his interview is that understanding market preferences and expectations is key to a successful brand. The right conversations up front with suppliers can accelerate the process of finding the right products.

Kevin of Camellia Sinensis gave a good overview of their client base and how they married their single-origin focus while satisfying their blended tea customers.

I have plenty of clients that drink something like an Earl Grey in the mornings and then a natural tea in the afternoon. Some of our clients prefer flavored tea while others prefer single origin teas.

We have a selection of flavored teas in our shop to help people new to our collection find a familiar place to start. For complete newcomers, a selection with flavors like strawberry, chocolate, pumpkin, and other tastes they know, makes initial interaction and selection easy. All you need to know is how long to leave it in the water.

Some of our clients stick with the blended teas forever and never move on to the single-origin. Others move on to explore teas with more specific, artisanal back-stories that require additional explaining or guidance.

Kevin understands their clientele and has worked to provide high quality teas in their shop, going to great lengths to source a curated assortment of blends that align with their brand mission.

This is also part of Marzi's role as a tea consultant. She works with restaurants, shops, hotels, and other businesses to align their products to their brand and regional preferences. In one instance, she was asked to make a chai blend for a company in the southwest United States.

Tailoring your specific flavoring profile to each market is an art in and of itself. A client asked me to help them make a chai spiced with a little hot chili. This works in their local market, but would not be accepted in other areas.

There are regional differences and preferences that you need to cater to. Not everyone bothers to hire a tea consultant, or to find out what their clients want or need. They do not consider what the regional passions are.

Unfortunately, when a brand does not do their due diligence to learn their customers' flavor expectations, their products might flop. And there are more considerations than just flavor.

Certifications, including organic, and other product information added to labels, are also something that customers will use to decide if they want to purchase tea from one brand or another. Every tea company should do their own research to figure out what types of certifications are appropriate. Also, they should adhere to any pertinent local health and safety laws, such as listing any allergies.

When I was speaking with Don, he said:

At the end of the day, we as tea industry professionals love the product. We advocate for tea. But we also have to be realistic that regardless of feelings, we are still running a business. Just like any other business in any industry, that means we must have sales.

Knowing our customers is the only way to make sales on tea. If your customer does not care about certifications and just wants the cheapest product, then that is what you need to create. If you are in an area that is very health conscious or 'woke,' you need to cater to that by considering various certifications such as organic or Fair Trade.

It does not matter how many certifications your product has, if it is not important to your customer, then you won't have sales. If you do not have sales, you do not have a business.

Customers need to be the focus of all brands, and delivering products that resonate with them will lead to sales. Regardless of any personal feelings towards certifications, if a brand's customers resonate with certain certifications, then they should make it part of their product assortment.

Every bit of information shared with the tea community will help drive growth in the tea industry. This resource is a testament to the collective passion that tea professionals share. There have been many people who have helped me personally grow in the industry, and this resource is one attempt to pay that forward to the next budding crowd of passionate tea professionals.

Thank you for taking the time to read this. I hope that you have learned about the blended tea industry and that your top questions were answered. If you have found value here, please leave a review or share it with someone you think might find it useful.

I would enjoy hearing from you if you have any questions, feedback, or if you just feel like talking tea. Please reach out to me on the following platforms:

Email: sirwillotleaf@gmail.com
Instagram: @sirwillotleaf
LinkedIn: William Dietz

www.ingramcontent.com/pod-product-compliance
Lightning Source LLC
Chambersburg PA
CBHW011315080526
44587CB00024B/4011